HEBREW IS EASY
Hebrew Basics:
From Alef to Shamar

YESHIAH YISRAEL

DEDICATION

To My Mother Niphla'ah Baht Asher

✝	'alep	'		𐤋	lamed	l
𐤁	bet	b		𐤌	mem	m
𐤂	gimel	g		𐤍	nun	n
𐤃	dalet	d		𐤎	samek	s
𐤄	he	h		𐤏	ayin	'
𐤅	waw	w		𐤐	pe	p
𐤆	zayin	z		𐤑	tsade	ṣ
𐤇	het	ḥ		𐤒	qop	q
𐤈	tet	ṭ		𐤓	reš	r
𐤉	yod	y		𐤔	šin	š
𐤊	kap	k		𐤕	taw	t

CONTENTS

Acknowledgments i

1 Introduction 1

2 The Alphabet & The Vowels 4

3 Simple Rules of Hebrew 15

4 Simple Understanding of Masculine Nouns 17

5 Simple Understanding of the Kal/Qal Stem 23

6 Conclusion 28

7 Bibliography 29

8 About The Author 30

ACKNOWLEDGMENTS

On the human level I acknowledge my mother, to whom this book is dedicated. The woman who helped me understand the Hebrew language. The woman who motivated me to want to study and who bought books for edification purposes.

I want to acknowledge Ema Miryom Baht Levi who since I was eight years old was shown as a teacher/morah in the Hebrew language and able to be approached by myself as a child to glean information.

I want to acknowledge Ema Shoshanah Baht Levi also who inspired me to write a book on Hebrew, having already written a book herself.

I want to acknowledge Ema Naami Baht Levi who inspired me to write and teach.

I want to acknowledge sister Tashaunda who supported and encouraged me to write this book.

I want to acknowledge, may he rest in peace now, Moreh Meshael Ben Yisrael who was a teacher, counsellor and instructor in Hebrew and in life.

I want to acknowledge, may he be blessed, Moreh Yehotsadek Ben Yisrael who was a person who taught Hebrew classes over 2-3 hours easy and made Hebrew make sense to me.

1
INTRODUCTION

To understand Hebrew, as with anything else, one must have an open mind and a willing heart. This book is not made for them who care to debate. This is made for them who have an interest in learning Hebrew. The author is a student of great Hebrew instructors in the Israelite community such as **Moreh Meshael** and **Moreh Hoshea**. The author does not claim to know everything and is open to constructive criticism.

Hebrew, as a language, in this book, will focus on two aspects. One being Biblical/Ancient and the other being Modern. It is important to state that modern Hebrew is basically ancient Hebrew put in modern usage. Example is the fact that *quarar* (קרר) means 'to cool' and by prefixing the letter Mem (מ) one gets *M'quarar* מְקָרֵר meaning 'refrigerator.' Another important aspect is the fact that Modern Hebrew is not Yiddish. Yiddish is a conglomerate of different European languages written in

1

Hebrew letters. The word Ahb (אָב) means 'father' in Hebrew. *Ahb* itself as you see is written in English letters, yet it is not an English word. The understanding of translation and transliteration too much be understood. A translation for instance of the word Mashal (מָשָׁל) in Hebrew is 'example'...the transliteration of the word *Yosehf* is Joseph. The meaning of *Yosehf* is adding/increasing. Thus, we can distinctly see a difference between translation and transliteration. In the Old Testament, we see Nebuchadnezzar who was a king in Babylon. His Babylonian name was *Nabû-kudurri-uṣur* and it meant Nabu protect my firstborn. Nebuchadnezzar though seen written in Hebrew נְבוּכַדְנֶאצַּר is not a Hebrew word.

My formal introduction into Hebrew came in the 1980's when I was a student and a child of an Israelite congregation called Kol Sh'aireit Bnai Yisrael in The Bronx, New York. After getting visual information on Hebrew my family went to another place in Brooklyn, New York, called B'nai Adath Kol Beit Yisrael. There I received the courage to want to learn the language. This comes from **Adon Aharon Ben Zevulon**. After that we attended a place called Hashabah Yisrael, in Queens, New York, under <u>Cohane Michael</u>, and from then on the knowledge of Hebrew was just very easy and I had a passion for learning it.

Hebrew like anything else, only comes to those who want it. If one puts the time, dedication and effort into learning, it will be learned.

This book is a guide. It is not intended for deep research, but rather as a guide for those who want to understand the easiness and simplicity of Hebrew.

The teachers whose names are bold typed are now deceased.

2
THE ALPHABET & THE VOWELS

The first letter of the Hebrew Alphabet is the letter Alef/Aleph. The meaning of Alef is 'clan, thousand.' The verb means 'to teach.'

The second letter of the Hebrew Alphabet is the letter Bet/Beth. The meaning of Bet is 'house, house of'. The letter Bet makes the B sound

The third letter of the Hebrew Alphabet is the letter Gimel. The meaning of Gimel is 'camel' and in the verb it means 'to deal.' The letter Gimel makes the G sound.

The fourth letter of the Hebrew Alphabet is the letter Dalet. The meaning of Dalet is a door. The letter Dalet makes the D sound

The fifth letter of the Hebrew Alphabet is the letter Heh/Hay. The meaning of Heh is 'behold'. The letter Heh makes the H sound.

The sixth letter of the Hebrew Alphabet is the letter Waw. The meaning of Waw is 'hook.' The letter Waw makes the W sound.

The seventh letter of the Hebrew Alphabet is the letter is the letter Zayin. The meaning of Zayin is 'weapon'. The letter Zayin makes the Z sound.

The eighth letter of the Hebrew Alphabet is the letter Khet. The meaning of Khet is 'fence'. The letter Khet makes the 'KH' sound.

The ninth letter of the Hebrew Alphabet is the letter Tet. The meaning of Tet is 'snake'. The letter Tet makes the T sound.

The tenth letter of the Hebrew Alphabet is the letter Yohd. The meaning of Yohd is 'hand.' The letter Yohd makes the Y sound.

The eleventh letter of the Hebrew Alphabet is the letter Kahf. The meaning of Kahf is palm. Spoon. The letter Kahf makes the K sound.

The twelfth letter of the Hebrew Alphabet is the letter Lamed. The meaning of Lamed is 'teach'. The letter Lamed makes the "L" sound.

The thirteenth letter of the Hebrew Alphabet is the letter Mem. The meaning of Mem is 'water'. The letter Mem makes the "M" sound.

The fourteenth letter of the Hebrew Alphabet is the letter Nun/Noon. The meaning of Nun is 'fish'. The letter Nun makes the "N" sound.

The fifteenth letter of the Hebrew Alphabet is the letter Samek. The meaning of Samek is 'support'. The letter Samek makes the "S" sound.

The sixteenth letter of the Hebrew Alphabet is the letter Ayin. The meaning of Ayin is 'eye'. The letter Ayin makes (according to some) a soft G like guttural sound. Some say Ayin is mute.

The seventeenth letter of the Hebrew Alphabet is the letter Peh. The meaning of Peh is 'mouth'. The letter Peh makes the P, some say F, sound.

ﬡ

The eighteenth letter of the Hebrew alphabet is the letter Tzade. The meaning of Tzade is 'fish-hook'. The letter

Tzade makes the 'TZ' sound.

The nineteenth letter of the Hebrew alphabet is the letter Quoof. The meaning of Quoof is 'monkey/ape'. The letter Quoof makes the 'Qu' sound.

The twentieth letter of the Hebrew Alphabet is the letter Resh. The meaning of Resh is head/leader. The letter Resh makes the R sound.

The twenty-first letter of the Hebrew alphabet is the letter Sheen. The meaning of Sheen is 'tooth'. The letter Sheen makes the 'Sh' sound.

The twenty-second letter of the Hebrew alphabet is the letter Taw/Thaw. The meaning of Taw/Thaw is 'sign'. The letter Taw/Thaw makes the T (some say TH sound).

In "modern" Hebrew using the Aramaic lettering as seen above, we have certain letters referred to as final letters. In many other cases, they are called the sofeet letters. There are five of them and ONLY appear at the end of the word.

This letter is called Kaf sofeet and makes the K sound at the end of words. This letter can be seen with a Sh'wah or with a Quamatz within it.

This letter is called a Mem sofeet and makes the M sound at the end of words. This letter is never accompanied by a vowel.

This letter is Noon Sofeet and makes the N sound at the end of words. This letter is sometimes accompanied with a vowel, only the Quamatz.

This letter is called Feh Sofeet and makes the P/F sound at the end of words. This letter is never accompanied by a vowel.

This letter is called Tzadeh/Tsadeh Sofeet and makes the Tz/Ts sound at the end of words. This letter is never accompanied by a vowel.

There are vowels in Hebrew and they are written as such:

These are shown below with the letter Heh

Patach- Under the letter- the AH sound- הַ

Quamatz- Under the letter- the AH sound- הָ (the quamatz with the letter Heh)

Segohl- Under the letter- the EH sound- הֶ

Tzareh- Under the letter- the AY sound- הֵ

Kheereeq- Under the letter- the EE sound- הִ

Qubootz- Under the letter- the OO sound- הֻ

Shuruk- Next to the letter-makes the oo sound הוּ

Kholam- Next to the letter- הוֹ (at times this is seen without the Waw)- making the 'OH' sound.

Sh'wa- Under the letter- A Sh'wa- This vowel here is a

special one. When the Sh'wa is with the first letter of any given word the sound of the letter is said. – הֱ

M'nasheh - מְנַשֶּׁה

The Sh'wa will never be at the beginning of the word that starts with a mute letter. Thus, you will not see a sh'wa with an Alef or an Ayin at the beginning of the word.

The Sh'wa will never be with the first and second letter of any word.

When a Sh'wa is with any letter that has a letter preceding it is absorbed with that letter. An example is as follows:

Yis'ra'el – יִשְׂרָאֵל

The Sh'wa is with the seen letter- שְׂ

Yeesh'quohd – יִשְׁקֹד

The Sh'wa is with the sheen letter

At times the Sh'wa can be with both the second and third letter of a word. An example is as follows:

Mal'k'kah- מַלְכְּךָ- your king

R'bee'ee רְבִיעִי- fourth

Malkut- מַלְכוּת- kingdom

A waw can be used as a vowel holder. The only two vowels that the waw hold are the "oh" and the oo sounds:

Shalom - שָׁלוֹם- peace

Ohyehb – אוֹיֵב- enemy

Ahrohn- אָרוֹן- closet

The waw that has a dagesh וֹ over it is called a Kohlam and makes the Oh sound. At times this sound is made without the Waw:

Bo בֹ (shown without the waw)

The waw can be used to hold the OO sound. This is called a Shuruq:

Oppressed - Ashooq - עָשׁוּק (shown with the waw)

Table – shulkhan - שֻׁלְחָן (shown without the waw)

Priesthood- K'hunat – כְּהֻנַּת (shown without the waw)

United- Koobar – חֻבָּר – (shown without the waw)

Another issue to consider is the matter of the Ai ("eye" in pronunciation).

Anytime a patch or a quamatz is with a letter and immediately followed by a Yohd the sound is Ai/Eye

Life- Khai -חַי

My lord- Adonai – אֲדֹנָי

Another matter is the matter of the Ahch (akh) sound at the end of a word.

When a Khet ח is the last letter of a word and it has a Patach with it חַ the sound of the Patach (ah) precedes the sound of the Khet.

Key – מַפְתֵּחַ- maf'tay'ahch

Apple – תַפּוּחַ- tapu'ahch

The Basic Pronouns

I – Ani - אֲנִי

You – Ata- אַתָּה

You (fem)- Aht אַת

He (he is)- Hoo- הוּא

She (She is)- Hee- הִיא

13

We (we are)- Anachnu- אֲנַחְנוּ

You (mp) (you are)- Atem   אַתֶּם

You (fp) (you are)- Aten אַתֶּן

They (m) (they are)- Hem הֵם

They (f) (they are)- Hen הֵן

3
SIMPLE RULES OF HEBREW

Hebrew is listed as an Afro-Asiatic language and is akin to Ethiopic, Kushitic, Arabic, Amharic, and Aramaic, as well as other languages, deemed Semitic by some. Hebrew is read from right to left.

The Modern Hebrew is made up of Asian (Western Asian) and slight European influences. The European influences can be seen in the pronunciation of Bet as Vet and Waw as Vav. The letter Seen in Hebrew is a variant of letter Sheen.

Many say that the vowels were written/placed by the Masorites in the 9/10th century A.D. However, as Josephus points out the Hebrew sounds are alike to the Aramaic sounds (*see Josephus, Antiquities of the Jews, Book 12, Chap. 2*). Since Aramaic has unwritten sounds (no seen vowels) we can surmise that Hebrew too had unwritten sounds/vowels. On page 19 are a few examples to show that Hebrew had to have sounds/unwritten vowels.

Whatever sound the letter makes is the sound it starts with. Thus, Bet makes the B sound. Zayin makes the Z sound. **Once one masters the alphabet and the sound of the vowels together then one knows how to read Hebrew.**

4
SIMPLE UNDERSTANDING OF
MASCULINE NOUNS

Masculine nouns are any noun that does not have the suffix of the Heh preceded by any letter that is accompanied by a Quamatz. For example:

Horse סוּס

Uncle דּוֹד

Feminine nouns in Hebrew are noted by the suffix of a Heh letter preceded by any letter that is accompanied by a Quamatz. Example:

Mare סוּסָה

Aunt דּוֹדָה

The plural in Hebrew is shown in most cases in the

masculine as eem (im) –םְי.

The plural in Hebrew is shown in most cases in the feminine as oht (ohth) וֹת

The letters Heh and Taw are feminine letters. Examples of feminine words are:

Torah תּוֹרָה   Queen-   -malkah- מַלְכָּה

Queens-malkoht- מַלְכֹות

Girl- נַעֲרָה -Na'arah   Girls – נַעֲרֹות- Na'aroth

Verbs which are feminine are as follows:

Shomrah שׁוֹמְרָה   Shomeret שׁוֹמֶרֶת

Verbs which are feminine plural are as follows:

Shohmroht שׁוֹמְרֹות

The Hebrew writing we see today in Torah Scrolls, the Dead-Sea Scrolls, and other literature are the Aramaic Alphabet. (*Source- 1. – Basics of Biblical Aramaic, Miles Pelt, 2011*)

Hebrew over the course of many years has not changed drastically from its original structure and meaning. (*Source- 2. – History of the Hebrew Language, Angel Saenze-Babillos, 1996*)

Most today are learning Hebrew over the age of 15 so many have to learn to read and write, then speak the language. That, however, is not a problem. A goal of this book is to help get the understanding of Hebrew to our people.

Hebrew, like any other language, has sound. Sound is made up of the vocal cords in one's throat. In literature, sounds are expressed in what is called vowels. Hebrew, as any other language has vowels.

Stranger – גֵּר

He dwelt- גָּר

Woman - אִשָּׁה

Fire Offering - אִשֶּׁה

Without different sounds/vowels there will be no distinction between the said above (and many more) words.

Regarding the rules of Hebrew, we must understand the grammar (Diqduq) of the language. There is a masculine and feminine in Hebrew. As my aforementioned teacher, Moreh Meshael, stated " Hebrew is the language of gender." The application of Proverbs 12:1 is important.

In colleges, they recommend that one does not take Hebrew classes while only knowing only English. One of the goals of this book is to show that Hebrew is easy and no other language is needed to understand how Hebrew is. However, it does help in the matter of grammar when one knows another language.

A noun is a person place or thing. The noun in Hebrew is the same. A noun can be in Hebrew with two or more syllables:

- Basket- sahl- סַל

- Rain- geshem- גֶּשֶׁם

- Boat-ahniya- אֳנִיָּה

- Faith- Emunah- אֱמוּנָה

- Frog- Tz'farday'a- צְפַרְדֵּעַ

A masculine noun is shown in possession- the word yad/yahd- hand:

- Hand- -yahd- יָד

- Your hand –yadeka --יָדְךָ

- Your hand (f) -yadayk- יָדֵךְ

- His hand – -yadoh -יָדוֹ

- Her hand-yadahh -יָדָהּ

- Our hand –yadeynu -יָדֵינוּ

- Your hand (masculine plural- speaking to more than one male)-yadkem- יָדְכֶם

- Your hand (feminine plural- speaking to more than one female-yadken -יָדְכֶן

- Their hand (masculine)-yadaham יָדָם

- Their hand (feminine)-yadahn יָדָן

A masculine noun, same as above, in the plural possessive form:

- My hands- יָדַי- yadai

- Your hands- יָדֶיךָ- yadeka

- Your hands (feminine)- יָדַיִךְ - yadaiyeek

- His hands- יָדָיו - yadiyw

- Her hands- יָדֶיהָ- yadehha

- Our hands-יָדֵינוּ - yadehnu

- Your hands (masculine plural)- יְדֵיכֶם- y'dehkem

- Your hands (feminine plural)- יְדֵיכֶן- y'dayken

- Their hands (masculine)-יְדֵיהֶם- y'dayhem

- Their hands (feminine) יְדֵיהֶן- y'dayhen

The above noun we discussed is a masculine noun.

5
SIMPLE UNDERSTANDING OF THE KAL/QAL STEM

There are seven (7) verb stems in Hebrew, however, we will deal with just the first stem in this book. The first stem is the Qual (qal) stem. The word Qual means 'easy.' Thus the name of this book.

A verb we will use is as follows- Shamar- שָׁמַר

The verb means 'to guard, watch, observe.'

In the present tense of said verb we see accompanied by the pronouns that go with them when speaking:

- Shohmer (ani, ata, hoo) - שֹׁמֵר

- Shohmeret (ani, aht, hee) שֹׁמֶרֶת

- Shohmreem (anachnu, atem, hem) שֹׁמְרִים

- Shohmroht (anachnu, aten, hen) שֹׁמְרוֹת

The pronouns can be said/written before or after the verb. The past tense of the same verb is as follows:

- Shamartee (said by ether male or female) -I guarded - שמרתי

- Shamarta (ata) – you guarded שמרת

- Shamart (aht)- you guarded (f) שמרת

- Shamar (hoo)- he guarded -שמר

- Shamrah (hee)- she guarded   שמרה-

- Shamarnu (anachnu)- we guarded   שמרנו-

- Shamartem (atem)- you guarded (mp) -שמרתם

- Shamarten (aten)- you guarded (fp) -שמרתן

- Shamru (hem/hen)- they guarded (m/f) -שמרו

The pronouns can be placed before or after the conjugated verb. The Future Tense is as follows:

- Eshmohr (ani- masculine or feminine) אשמר- I will watch

- *Teeshmohr (ata) תשמור- You will watch (masc)

- Teeshm'ree (aht) תשמרי – You will watch (fem)

- Yeeshmohr (hoo) ישמר- He will watch

- *Teeshmohr (hee) תשמר- She will watch

- Neeshmohr (anachnu) נשמר- We will watch

- Teeshm'ru (atem) תשמרו- You will watch (mp)

- Teeshmohrna (aten) תשמרנה- You will watch (fp)**

- Yeesh'm'ru (hem) ישמרו- They will watch

- Teeshmohrna (hen) תשמרנה- They will watch (fem) **

*We should note that the second person masculine singular and the third person feminine singular is the same word in the future tense.

**We should note that the second person feminine plural and third person feminine plural in Hebrew is the same word in the future tense.

In dealing with the stance of the book, we want to explain that in Hebrew there is such a thing as a participle for the previous verbs (and those that follow that pattern). Another example is with the verb Shamar:

- Shamur watched/guarded-שמור

- Sh'murah watched/guarded (fs)-שמורה

- Sh'mureem (mp) watched/guarded-שמורים

- Sh'muroht watched/guarded (fp) -שמורות

- One can say-Ani Shamur I am watched- אני שמור

- One can say-Ani Sh'murah I am -אני שמורה watched (f)

Other examples:

- Anachnu Sh'mureem – We are watched אנחנו שמורים

- Anachnu Sh'muroht – We are watched (feminine plural) אנחנו שמורות

There is also an imperative. The imperative is the command form. This is formed by such:

- Sh'mohr- watch! – this is when you are speaking to one male שמור

- Sheemree- watch! – this is when you are speaking to one female שמרי

- Sheemru- watch! – this is when you are speaking to just males or mixed company- שמרו

- Sh'mohrna- watch! – this is when you are speaking to just females- שמרנה

Also, there is what is called a gerund in Hebrew. A gerund is from a verb that acts as a noun. This is as follows:

- Beeshmohr- In/with watching בשמור

- Keeshmohr- like/as watching כשמר

- Leeshmohr- to watch/for watching לשמר

- Meeshmohr- from watching משמר

This is the model form of the verb that is followed by like verbs when conjugated:

- Write- Katab- כתב

- Meet- Pagash פגש

- Sell- Makar מכר

- Remember- Zakar זכר

6
CONCLUSION

As stated the book is intended on the light/easy aspect. It is not intended for deep research. This is a book which was dedicated to helping spread the knowledge of Hebrew to the masses. There will be other books of this nature in the future. I can be contacted at 908-587-4841 or Kashubhut@gmail.com

For video understanding of this booklet, go to:

Youtube channel- Moreh Yeshiah Hebrew Lessons

Type- Hebrew Class 5, review of lessons 1-4
https://www.youtube.com/watch?v=se498U7c7bY

Type- Hebrew Lesson 6- the explanation of the vowels in detail-
https://www.youtube.com/watch?v=gK3a5OKJKjc

7
BIBLIOGRAPHY

Biblical Hebrew, Page H. Kelly, 1992

Biblical Archeology in Focus, Keith Schoville, 1978

A History of the Hebrew Language, Angel Badillos 1993

201 Hebrew Verbs, Abraham Hilkin, 1970

English Hebrew- Hebrew English Dictionary, Ehud Yehudah, 1989

Hebrew and English Lexicon of the Old Testament, William Gesenius, 1907

ABOUT THE AUTHOR

Moreh Yeshiah, in giving honor to the Creator of heaven and earth, the author wants to say Todah Y-H for the release of this book. Starting to study Hebrew at age 13, though introduced to it at age 4, I wanted to learn what I can.

Inspired by the situation with Joseph and his brothers in Genesis, the interpreter is what convinced me that language was important. Having sat under great teachers in Hebrew (who were black) and given free books from schoolteachers (who were white) I began by age 14 to just study from the 201 Hebrew verbs book. I studied grammar and Hebrew syntax and realized that the language was part of a Western Asian/North African language, not a European language.

I began teaching Hebrew at age 18 in a congregation called Khalutzay Yisrael. At age 26 at a congregation called Machaneh Yehudah. It was, however, at age 37 I took the old Hebrew notes from age 15 and composed this book you have in your hand.

For good quality and durable styled clothing contact Mr. Salazar at Praverbnyc.com

For an excellent book on the Hebrew language, a book that inspired me to write this book. Contact Ema Shoshanah Levi @ Sholevi@aol.com

For healthy drinks that taste great contact Ema Athaliah @ Athaliahsbeverages@gmail.com.

I can vouch the drinks are worth the investment.

Made in the USA
Las Vegas, NV
15 September 2023